Anger Management Workbook for Kids

101 Playful Activities Helping Children to Diffuse Tension, Build Awareness, and Retake Command of Their Emotions

Table of Contents

Introduction to the Parent

Dear Parent,

All parents love their children more than anything in the world. They want to see them happy and flourishing. However, living with an angry child isn't easy. You don't only have to deal with the constant tantrums, but it is also heartbreaking to see your child miserable. However, for every problem, there is a solution. This book will provide all the information you need to help your child, including interesting exercises, techniques, and activities to get their anger under control.

The book begins by defining anger and what triggers this feeling in your child. It will then explain how anger expresses itself and that your child can only regulate it by trying to understand it rather than deny or dismiss it. No one gets angry without reason. The book will guide your child to understand the source of their anger and why they experience different feelings. The book also discusses different types of thoughts and how they can influence emotions.

Fear is powerful, and it can impact both thoughts and emotions. The book will explain the concept of fear – and why it can sometimes be a helpful feeling.

The next part of the book will focus on activities like meditation and breathing exercises that your child can practice regulating their anger. You will also find effective techniques to teach your child to speak up and express their feelings. The book will also discuss how your child can overcome negative thoughts and change their inner narrative.

The last part of the book will focus on creative and fun habits that your child can add to their daily routine to keep them calm. It will also explain the concept of letting go and how forgiving and forgetting is better than holding on to resentment.

All the techniques in this workbook are effective, and the more your child practices them, the calmer they will become. Many of them are fun – like drawing – which they will definitely enjoy. If they struggle with other exercises like meditation, you can encourage them by practicing with them. You can also use rewards to get them interested in the book and to follow all the tips mentioned here.

Introduction to the Child

Dear _____,

Anger isn't always a bad feeling, even though you don't like being angry because screaming hurts your throat – and it upsets mom and dad, too.

Everyone gets angry, and you have every right to express your feelings. However, anger can be tricky and controlling how you behave in certain situations. Don't worry; you have it in you to keep this emotion under control. Just like superheroes beating bad guys, you can also beat your anger. This book will explain everything to you, like why you get angry and how to remain calm whenever you feel like you are about to explode. There are also many fun activities in this book that you can do each time you feel angry that will keep you calm and relaxed.

Anger is like a monster, but not an evil one. Once you really understand it, you can be friends and live with it. Just like the Hulk, you will learn how to keep the green monster in control. Are you curious about meeting your anger monster? Are you ready to be best friends with it? Do you want to draw and learn fun things to do to be calm and happy? Keep reading.

Section 1: Why Am I Angry?

Why am I angry? That's a very interesting question. Before answering, you should first understand what anger is. Anger is a strong but normal reaction that all people feel, even grown-ups. You usually feel it when things go wrong, someone hurts your feelings, or does or says something you don't like. For example, if your best friend was supposed to come over and then canceled at the last minute because they wanted to do something with their brother or sister. You may feel angry.

There are many other emotions that you can feel when you are angry, like stress, irritation, and frustration. It is okay to feel angry from time to time, but if you always feel this way and can't control it, it can hurt you and your family and friends.

Anger Triggers

A trigger is anything that happens around you, like a smell or sound that brings bad memories, which can upset or anger you. Every person has different triggers. In other words, people get angry for different reasons. For instance, you may get angry if your brother plays with your toys, while someone else might get mad if someone wakes them from their nap.

So, to answer the big question, why do I get angry? You get angry because of how you feel about certain situations. There isn't a right or wrong reason to feel angry; everyone has the right to feel how they feel. In some cases, anger can also be necessary and healthy when you express it in a wise way. It can only be an issue when it is more frequent and out of control. Soon enough, you will learn interesting techniques to control your rage.

Exercises

1. Play this game with your sibling or your parent by acting out what anger looks, feels, or sounds like, and let the other person guess which one you are making. For example, stand and clench your fist and see if your mom or brother/sister notices what you are doing.Try to barely show the feeling, making it harder for them to guess. Or you might trick them by acting out more than one anger expression and see if they will guess them all.

LOOKS LIKE

- Red face
- Scrunched eyebrows
- Clenched fists
- Clenched jaws
- Tense lips
- Showing teeth
- Intense looks

FEELS LIKE

- Annoyed
- Upset
- Irritated
- Nervous
- Frustrated
- Resentful

SOUNDS LIKE

- Shouting
- Screaming
- Growling
- Rapid breathing

2. Where do you feel angry?

Show what a good artist you are! Draw a person and color in the circle below, and make them red in the parts where you feel angry the most, like your chest or stomach.

3. Check the words that match how you express your anger. Don't feel guilty for any of your choices. Everyone expresses their feelings in some way, and you are here to get better.

☐ Scream.
☐ Cry
☐ Throw things
☐ Bite
☐ Hit someone
☐ Lying on the floor and crying or screaming

4. Choose what other feelings you have when you are angry.

| Sad | Frustrated | Annoyed | Guilty | Humiliated | Hurt |

5. Now that you understand what anger triggers are, check the ones that apply to you.

☐ When my feelings get hurt
☐ Someone says "no" to me
☐ My parents/siblings turn off my video games
☐ Someone takes my stuff
☐ Waking up early to go to school
☐ Someone interrupts me when I am talking

☐ Hunger
☐ Doing my homework
☐ When I am talking but no one is listening to me
☐ Losing a game
☐ When someone is being unfair to me.

6. Draw what you think you look like when you get angry. Be as creative as you want.

7. Draw how you look when you are calm and happy, and look at the difference between the two.

8. Draw what your triggers look like or how you imagine they look like.

9. Drow a place where you feel calm and happy.

10. If your anger was a comic book bad guy, which one would it be? Draw it here.

Angry Monster Checker

HOW ANGRY IS YOUR MONSTER RIGHT NOW?

☐ Extremely angry   ☐ Fairly angry   ☐ Not sure   ☐ A little angry   ☐ Not angry

Section 2: Meeting My Anger Monster

Every person is different. Some people cry when they are sad, while others just stay quiet. Similarly, there are people who scream, shout, and throw things when they are angry, while others talk about how they are feeling and try to fix their problems. Here are the different types of anger. Do you know which one you usually use to express your frustrations?

Behavioral Anger

Behavioral anger is when you express yourself physically, often in a violent or fighting kind of way. You aren't usually in control of your emotions and may hurt the people around you. You don't do this on purpose, and you feel bad afterward. For instance, you can throw your toys at your brothers or sisters (we call those "siblings"), break your stuff, or even hit them.

Verbal Anger

Verbal anger is when you hurt someone using words to blame, disapprove of, or threaten them. You never mean to hurt the people you love, and you always feel guilty and say you're sorry once you calm down.

Passive Aggressive Anger

You can express yourself using *passive aggression* when you don't want to talk about your anger. Instead of fighting or facing the other person, you keep your feelings hidden. You will express them by either making fun of them or giving them the silent treatment. If the other person notices you are acting differently, you will usually say that nothing is wrong. This type is just as bad as shouting or hitting because it hurts the other person.

Don't feel guilty; there are ways you can express your anger without hurting the ones you love.

Chronic Anger

Chronic anger is feeling frustrated and angry toward your family, friends, and even yourself all the time. This type of anger can affect your relationships and schoolwork.

Overwhelmed Anger

With this type, your anger will feel out of control. It usually happens when you are very upset about something and don't know what to do. You can experience this feeling if you have an exam that you didn't prepare for and you feel sad and worried.

Retaliatory Anger

Retaliatory anger is what you do or say when someone is rude to you or upset you. This usually makes things worse. For instance, your classmate says something that makes you angry. Instead of ignoring them and being the better person, you insult them back and get in trouble.

Making Friends with My Anger

Your anger isn't your enemy; in fact, you can be friends with it. It is part of who you are. If you are afraid or ashamed of it, it will not go away; it will make the situation worse. You should understand that anger isn't a bad feeling and can sometimes be helpful. You must change your relationship with it and make it your new best friend, just like the Hulk and Bruce Banner.

Don't Be Mad at Anger

Since it's a negative emotion, you probably hate it whenever you feel this way. You usually feel guilty when you see your mom upset after you yell at her or when your sibling cries after you hit them. As a result, you get mad at anger and tell yourself that your feelings are wrong.

The trick is to accept it and understand there is nothing wrong with it. The problem isn't with your anger but with *how you express it*. Once you understand that, you will see that there is nothing wrong with getting angry every now and then.

Ask Your Anger Questions

Instead of treating your anger like a monster that should be avoided, think of it as another person inside you – try to get to know it better. Try to find out why you feel this way and what triggered this emotion. Get curious about your anger, get to know it, and make it your friend. Ask yourself, how long has your anger been around? This can bring bad memories that can be upsetting, and you could find that your anger has been protecting you from sadness and pain. Although this won't be easy, it is needed to have a better understanding of your anger and get it under control.

Exercises

Each person has an anger monster inside of them that often comes out during intense situations. It's okay, don't be afraid of it. It isn't evil, and most of the time, it just needs a big hug. Close your eyes and imagine your anger monster before you start these exercises.

11. Draw what your anger monster looks like.

12. Give your anger monster a name.

13. Say that name out loud a few times until you feel like you know it.

14. Now that you have become friends with your anger monster write the thoughts it has when it's angry.

15. Now, write how it feels when it's angry.

----

16. Draw what makes your anger monster super angry.

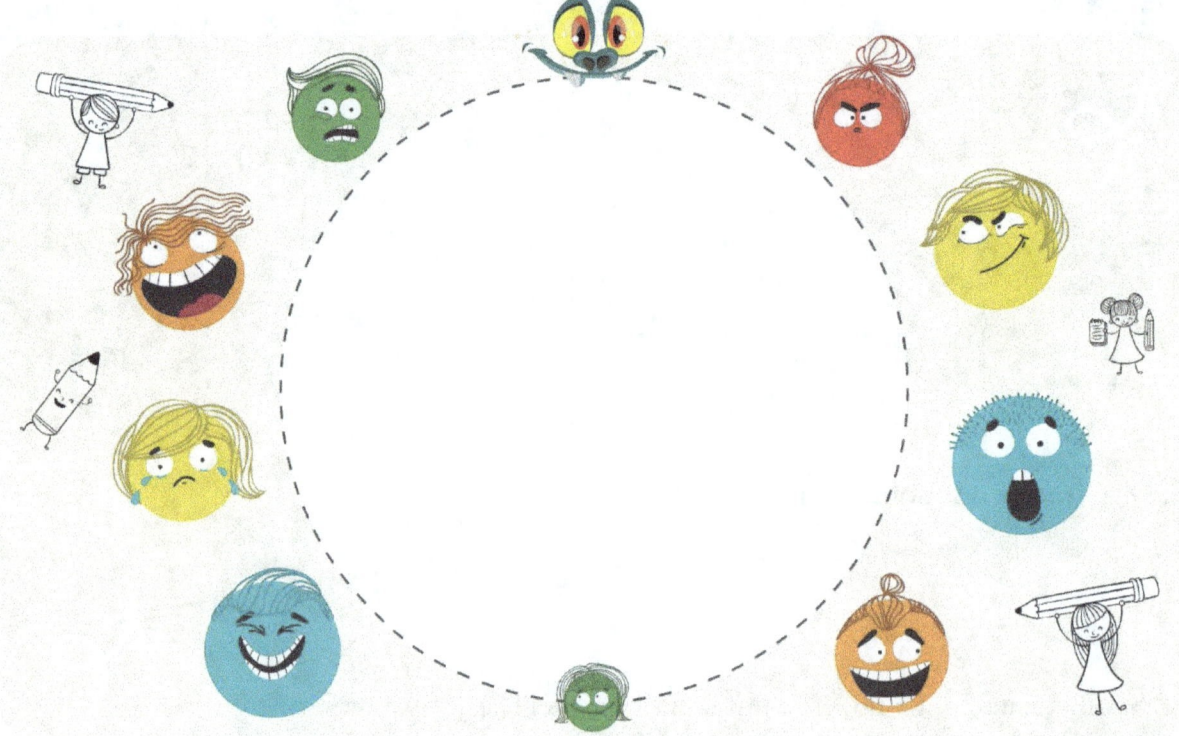

17. Draw places where your anger monster shows up.

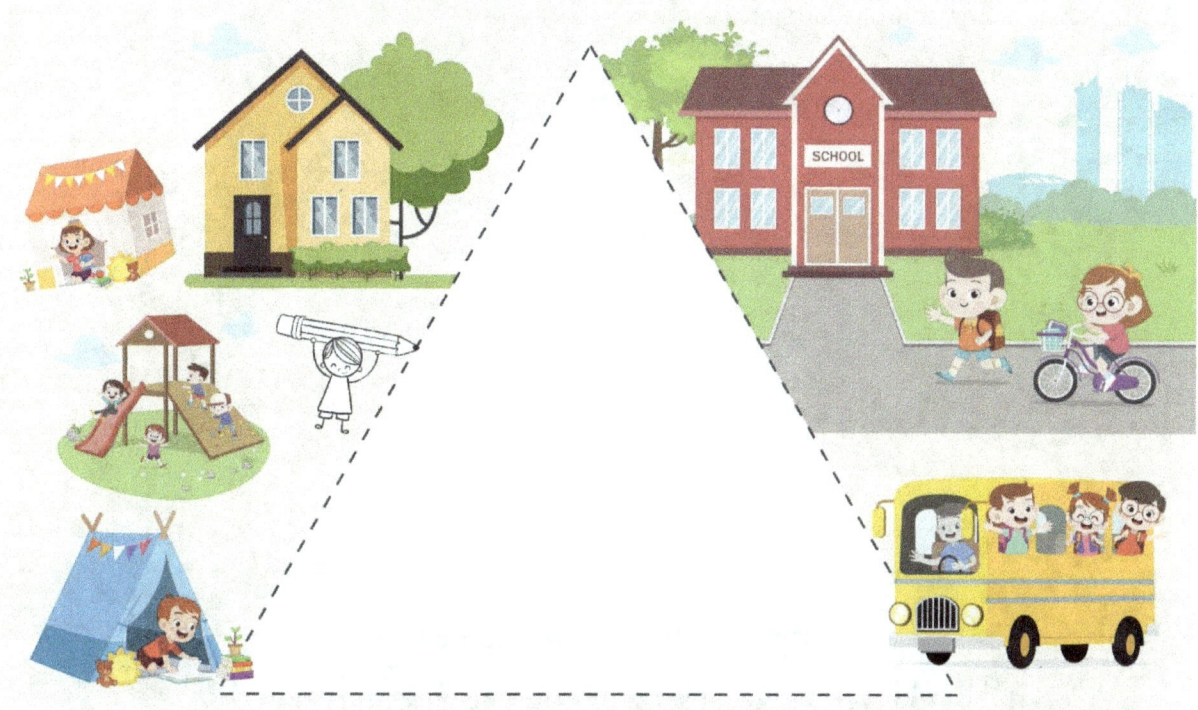

18. Draw how your anger monster reacts when it is angry. (Does it scream, throw things, or sit quietly?)

19. Close your eyes and imagine giving your angry monster a big hug.

20. Now, draw how it looks like after the hug.

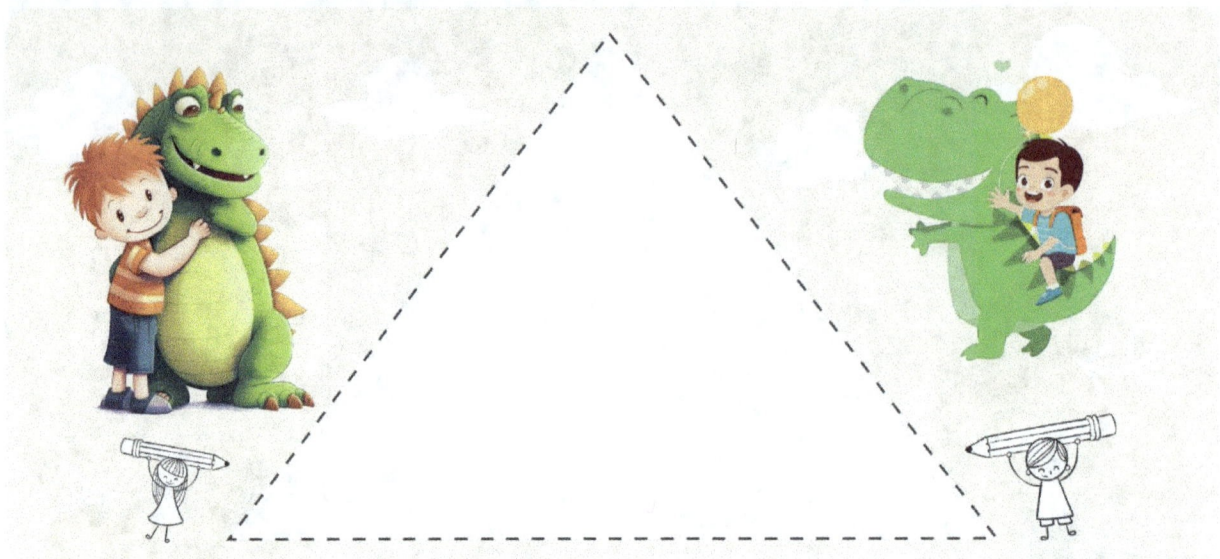

Angry Monster Checker

HOW ANGRY IS YOUR MONSTER RIGHT NOW?

| Extremely angry | Fairly angry | Not sure | A little angry | Not angry |

Section 3: The Emotions Detective: Getting to Know My Feelings

In this section, you will be like Sherlock Holmes and play detective to discover where your anger monster comes from. Anger usually comes from your emotions. In fact, sometimes, you aren't really angry but sad. Instead of crying or admitting you are hurt, you find it easier to be angry.

Emotions can be confusing, but you can learn to use your Sherlock Holmes abilities to better understand how you are feeling. For example, sometimes, you can be so angry that you start crying.

If you dig deep, you will realize that you are actually sad. Some emotions can be so powerful that they turn to anger, like fear, sadness, or hurt. It can be difficult to admit that you are afraid – or your feelings are hurt – so you find it easier to express yourself with anger.

Whenever you feel angry, try to find out the source. Like a real detective, look for clues to find the emotion that triggered your feelings.

There is a reason behind each emotion; they aren't random. They can often act as mechanisms (what causes it) for something. An emotional *mechanism* is something happening in your head where one emotion is switched to another, like when sadness turns into anger.

For example, your dad works far away, and you are excited to see him coming home for Christmas. However, your mom tells you that he won't be able to make it because he is stuck at work. You feel very angry, but if you dig deep, you will find that you are actually sad and disappointed.

To better understand your anger, you need to discover the emotions:

- You don't talk about it
- You don't feel comfortable with it
- You experience every day
- You try to hide

Expressing Your Feelings Without Anger

You can express your feelings without anger using these simple tips

- Use positive words when you talk about yourself out loud or in your head
- Listen to what the other person is saying before speaking
- Forgive others instead of being mad at them
- Accept the things you can't control.
- Write down or draw how you feel in your journal
- Accept all your emotions, even anger

Exercises

21. To better understand your anger, you need to discover what emotions:

- You don't talk about
- You don't feel comfortable with
- You experience day-to-day life
- You try to hide

Draw the emotions in the heart below.

22. Color this emotional detective based on how you are feeling right now.

23. Imagine your sibling or friend breaking your favorite toy, then draw the emotion you feel.

24. Draw your favorite three emotions.

25. Draw your three least favorite emotions.

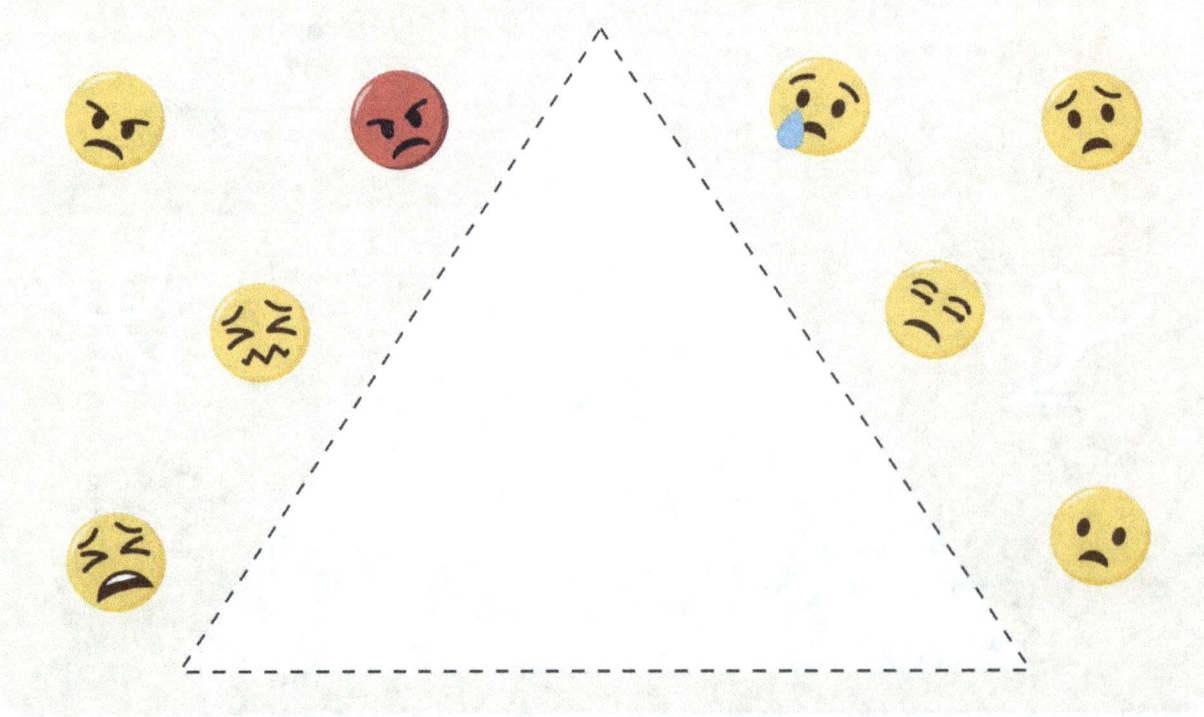

26. Draw how you feel when someone hurts your feelings and label it (whether it's anger, sadness, frustration, etc.)

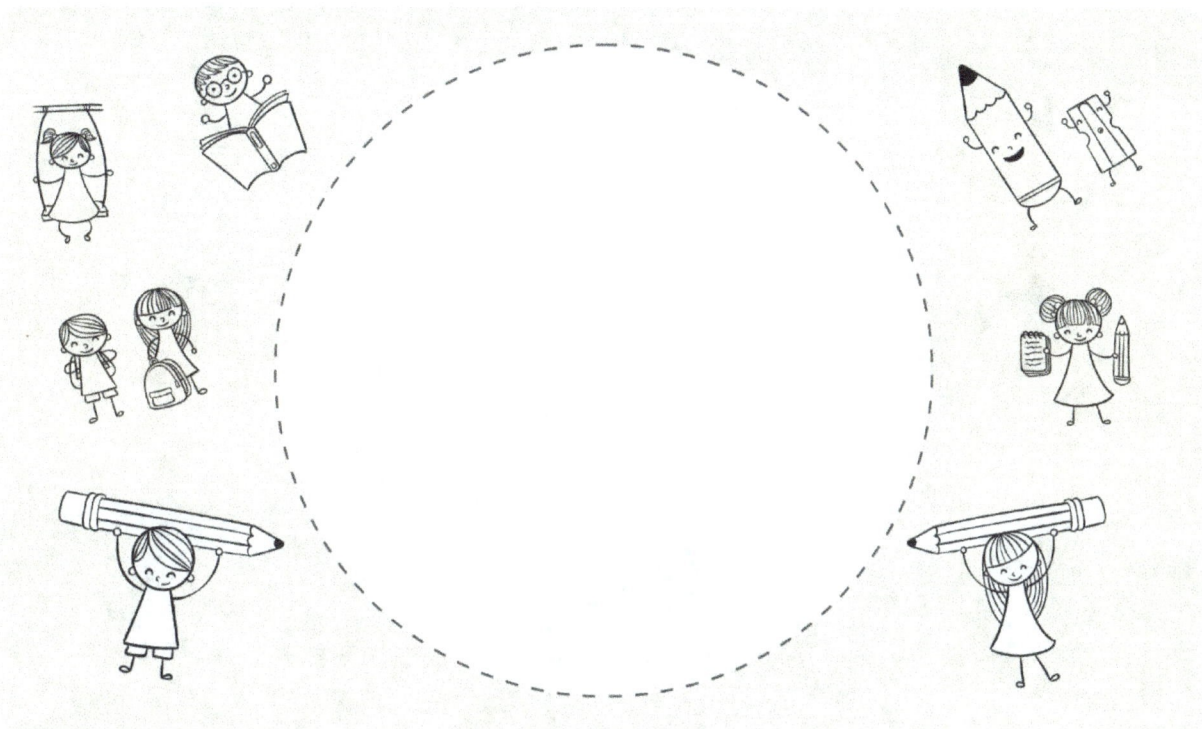

27. Which one of these is angry, and which one is sad?

28. Draw the emotion you wish to never experience again.

29. Draw a person you can be vulnerable with – that means you feel safe with them. You can tell them how you feel.

30. Draw your angry monster when it is feeling sad.

Angry Monster Checker

HOW ANGRY IS YOUR MONSTER RIGHT NOW?

☐ ☐ ☐ ☐ ☐

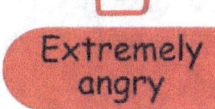 Extremely angry
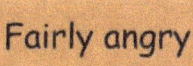 Fairly angry
 Not sure
 A little angry
 Not angry

Section 4: The Thought Detective: Getting to Know My Thoughts

Emotions can come from your thoughts. Different types of thoughts can affect how you feel about yourself and the world around you.

Negative Thoughts

Negative thinking is when you have bad and harmful thoughts about yourself, your life, and your family and friends. It is normal to have these thoughts every once in a while. However, when your thoughts are always negative, and you only focus on the bad things in life and ignore the positive, this can lower your self-esteem and make you sad and angry all the time.

Negative thoughts can also affect your school work and relationships with your family and friends. They can trigger many harmful emotions like sadness, guilt, frustration, anxiety, and anger.

Understand that these thoughts aren't real; your brain is playing tricks on you by telling you that you aren't good, smart, or funny enough. This can lead to self-blame, labeling yourself with negative words like "bad in sports." You might start feeling like nothing will ever go right and assume that everyone you meet is thinking negatively of you.

Repetitive Thoughts

Repetitive thoughts are constantly thinking about a situation, person, or idea. It is normal to sometimes think about something constantly and struggle to get it out of your head. However, when these thoughts become obsessive (you can't stop having them) and interfere with your daily life, this can be a problem.

Beliefs

Some beliefs can be destructive, like "I am not good enough," "I am not smart enough," or "Nobody likes me." They are negative thoughts that, with time, turn into beliefs that are impossible to shake off. They become part of who you are, and you believe these thoughts to be facts that can destroy your self-esteem (how you feel about yourself). When you believe you aren't good enough, you will be resentful and lash out at everyone you know.

Limiting Thoughts

Limiting thoughts convinces you of certain ideas you believe to be true. You can have these thoughts about yourself, school, or friends. For example, you hate math, so you believe that you will never get a good grade no matter how hard you study. These thoughts aren't real and can harm your life and keep you from doing things to get better. They will prevent you from achieving your goals because you have convinced yourself you don't have what it takes.

Limiting thoughts can protect you from disappointments and failure. For example, you tried out for the soccer team once but weren't accepted. You believe you will never be good enough to join the team, so you never try again. These thoughts are meant to protect you from further disappointments but often limit your possibilities.

Just like emotions, your thoughts are tools that you can use to get to the root of your anger.

Exercises

31. Do you experience negative thoughts, negative beliefs, or limiting thoughts? Write your answers on the brain illustration below.

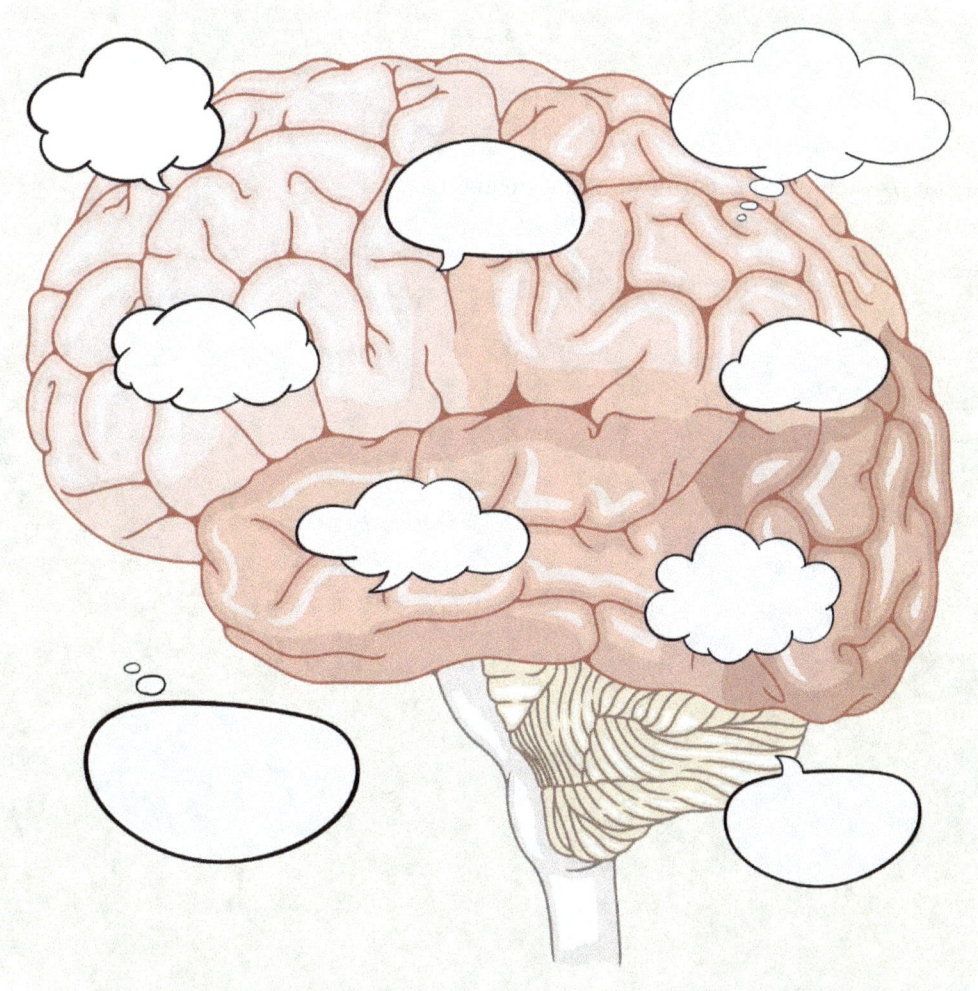

32. Draw your negative thoughts.

33. Draw how you feel when you have these thoughts.

34. Draw your angry monster when it has negative thoughts.

35. Write down a negative thought, then replace it with a positive thought in the boxes below.

36. Stand in front of a mirror and smile for a few seconds. Does your mood change?

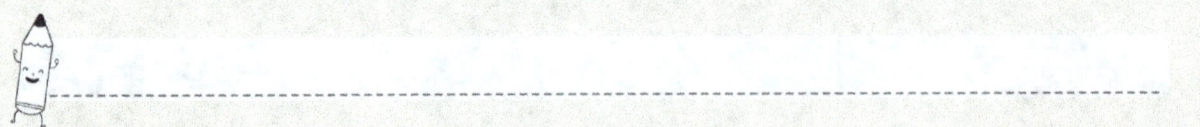

----

37. Draw a cute little monster running after your negative thoughts so it can eat them and free you from them.

38. Write three things you love about yourself. Use these to challenge the negative thoughts.

----

39. Draw how your angry monster will look once you stop thinking negatively.

40. Draw what your life will feel like without negative thoughts and beliefs.

Angry Monster Checker

HOW ANGRY IS YOUR MONSTER RIGHT NOW?

☐ ☐ ☐ ☐ ☐

| Extremely angry | Fairly angry | Not sure | A little angry | Not angry |

Section 5: Find the Fear: What Am I Afraid of?

Fear is one of the most common emotions in the universe. Everyone experiences this feeling, even the bravest people in the world – like Batman. You usually feel afraid when someone threatens you, whether emotionally or physically. Although fear is often considered a negative emotion, it is necessary for your survival. Fear pushes you to protect yourself when in danger and to be careful at all times.

One of the first emotions human beings learn is fear. This isn't a bad thing, as it keeps you safe from a very young age. This is why you would run if you saw a lion and would never put your hand in a fire because you know you will get hurt. Fear can be healthy when it saves your life.

However, it can be unhealthy when it puts negative thoughts in your head and holds you back in life. For example, you believe if you speak up in class, the other kids will laugh at you. This can create negative thoughts, making you sad and isolated (separated or apart from) from your classmates. These feelings will build up over time, leading to anger and frustration. However, if you face your fear and speak up in class, you will realize these thoughts are only in your head.

Face your fears to overcome the negative thoughts and emotions that impact your anger.

Exercise

41. Draw a big fear you have. (Don't be scared while doing this exercise; you put your fear on paper to get it out of your brain!)

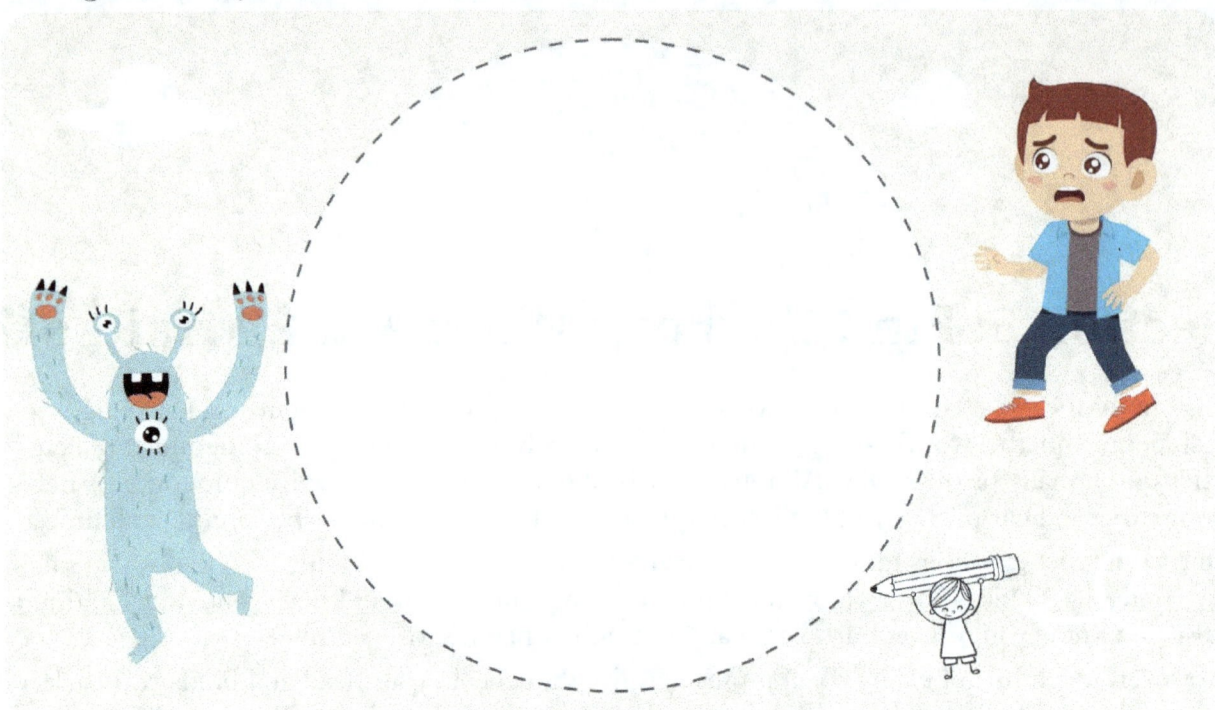

42. Draw what does your fear look like?

43. Imagine yourself as a superhero fighting your fears. Now draw it

44. Draw how you or your life will look like without fear.

45. Draw your anger monster when it's afraid.

46. Write down next to the fear thermometer your fears from your most scary to your least scary.

47. Laugh at your fears. Look at each fear and try to laugh out loud. This can reduce its effect on you and make you realize that they aren't as scary as you think.

48. Draw a picture to show how you feel after laughing at the face of your fears.

49. Write your fears on a piece of paper, tear it up, and blow it in the air. Do this activity in your backyard.

50. Now, as you are letting go of your fears, sing "Let it Go" by Elsa out loud.

Angry Monster Checker

HOW ANGRY IS YOUR MONSTER RIGHT NOW?

☐	☐	☐	☐	☐
Extremely angry	Fairly angry	Not sure	A little angry	Not angry

Section 6: Breathing and Mindfulness

Now that you understand where your anger comes from, it is time to take steps to get this emotion under control. In this section, you will find breathing exercises and ways to meditate to help reduce your anger and calm you down.

Meditation

Meditation is an ancient practice that people of all ages can do to keep them focused and relaxed. It can reduce stress, anxiety, and anger to keep you calm. It can also keep you focused, which is a necessary skill to beat your anger monster. When you are mindful (aware) of the present moment, you will also be aware of your feelings and quickly notice when you are angry and take control of your emotions so you can respond differently.

Now, you will learn some interesting meditation techniques to control your anger. Make sure to follow all the instructions. All meditation exercises should take place in a quiet room away from distractions.

51. Technique #1

Instructions:

1. Sit up straight in a comfortable position and close your eyes.
2. Breathe in and out slowly and deeply.
3. Forget about the world around you and only focus on your breathing.
4. Count each time you breathe in and out.
5. If you start daydreaming, slowly refocus on your breathing.
6. Keep doing this technique for five minutes or longer if you feel comfortable.

52. Technique #1

Instructions:

1. Sit in a comfortable position and close your eyes.
2. Take a few deep breaths.
3. Imagine all your negative thoughts and all the things that bother you are written or drawn with chalk.

4. Now imagine them all erased.

5. Keep watching as they all fade away one by one.

6. Allow your body and mind to relax.

Technique #3

Instructions:

Anger makes your body and head feel hot, but his meditation technique can cool you down.

1. Close your eyes and imagine you are holding a big cup of chocolate milkshake with a long purple straw in your hands.

2. Hold the cup close to your lips and take a long sip from the cup.

3. Take a deep breath while imagining you are drinking from the straw.

4. Close your mouth and exhale from your nose.

5. Keep imagining you are drinking from your smoothie while breathing until you feel calm.

53. Technique #4

Instructions:

1. Close your eyes and take a long and deep breath through your nose that fills your tummy.

2. As soon as you feel your tummy is filled with air, exhale from your mouth (like a dragon) while saying "Haaa," letting the anger and the negative emotions out.

3. Take another long and deep breath, but make your "Haaa" louder and longer this time.

4. Repeat this exercise until your anger goes away.

54. Technique #5

Instructions:

1. Close your eyes, or if you prefer, place your hands over them.

2. Breathe in and out, clear your mind, and let your body relax.

3. You feel free and are only focused on the present moment.

4. Imagine your anger monster is in a cave, and you are standing at the cave's entrance.

5. Your anger monster is very angry, and fire is coming out of its mouth like a dragon. You can see the smoke coming out of the cave.

6. Try to find out why your anger monster is angry. Ask yourself if something recently happened that annoyed you and made you mad.

7. You are the only person who knows why your anger monster is mad. Only you can control and calm it down if it gets out.

8. Think about the last few days and find the event that made your anger monster feel this way. Has something happened at school? Has your sibling taken one of your toys? Has your best friend said something that hurt your feelings?

9. While trying to find the reason, imagine you have drawn your anger monster out of the cave. Remember, you are the one in control.

10. Your anger monster is coming out of the cave.

11. You can imagine your anger monster as a female or male, or big or small.

12. Your anger monster is throwing a fit. Tell it you are here to take care of it and make it feel better.

13. Your anger monster sits down, pouting and breathing steam.

14. Approach it slowly, ask what it needs, and listen carefully.

15. It says it needs a hug.

16. Give your anger a big hug and feel its anger melt away.

17. Now, look at your anger monster. If it feels better, let it go back to sleep. If it doesn't, keep asking it what it needs until it calms down. It might need to know that you are okay or need to vent about why it's angry. It might simply need to know that you love it.

18. After your anger monster calms down, say goodbye and let it sleep in the cave.

19. Whenever you feel your anger monster waking up, return to its cave and help it get better.

Breathing Exercises

Anger makes you breathe faster – like you have been running or playing a sport. Breathing exercises (taking deep and slow breaths) will help calm you down.

55. Technique #1

INSTRUCTIONS:

1. Close or open your eyes (whatever makes you comfortable).

2. Move your tongue on top of your mouth and keep it closed.

3. Take a long, deep breath from your nose while counting to four

4. Hold it for seven seconds

5. Breathe out from your mouth for eight seconds

56. Technique #2

INSTRUCTIONS:

1. Sit comfortably on the floor and turn your hands into a fist.

2. Breathe in while lifting one fist over your head.

3. Breathe out while making a growling sound, then bring down your fist and raise the other one.

4. Keep repeating this "gorilla motion" until you calm down.

58. Technique #3

INSTRUCTIONS:

1. Breathe in from your nose and raise your hands over your head while standing.

2. Bring your palms together while still over your head.

3. Imagine yourself standing tall like a mountain.

4. You are standing strong while your feet are like roots holding you to the ground.

5. Breathe out through your mouth and place your palms in front of your chest.

6. Repeat this exercise five times.

59. Technique #4

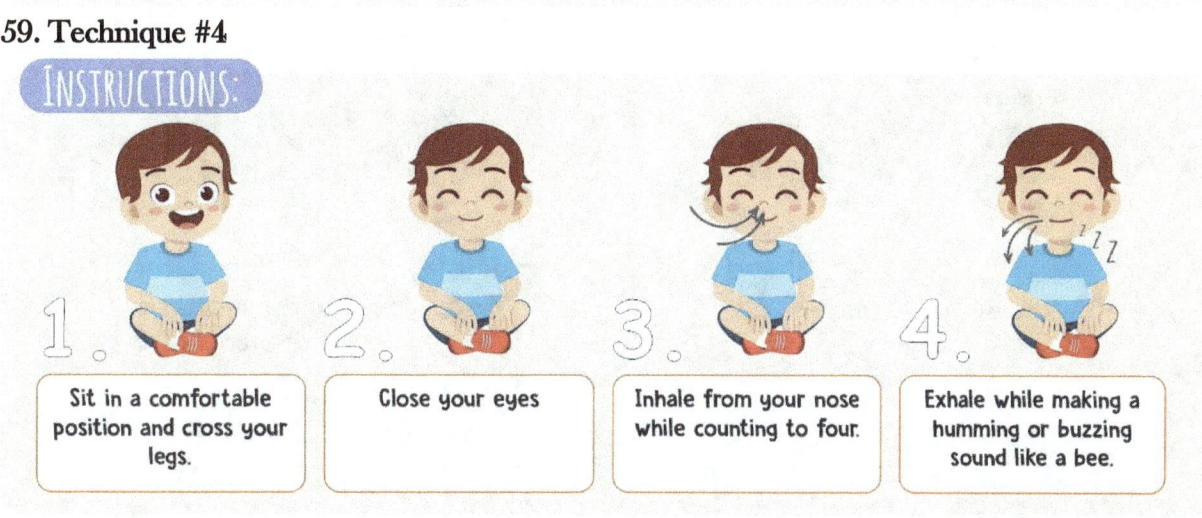

INSTRUCTIONS:

1. Sit in a comfortable position and cross your legs.

2. Close your eyes

3. Inhale from your nose while counting to four.

4. Exhale while making a humming or buzzing sound like a bee.

60. Technique #5

1. Lie down and place your favorite toy over your tummy.

2. Breathe in deeply while counting to three.

3. Breathe out while counting to four.

4. Watch your toy rise and fall on your tummy with every breath.

5. Repeat five to ten times.

Angry Monster Checker

HOW ANGRY IS YOUR MONSTER RIGHT NOW?

☐ ☐ ☐ ☐ ☐

| Extremely angry | Fairly angry | Not sure | A little angry | Not angry |

Section 7: Speaking Up and Expressing Myself

Speaking up is the ability to calmly express your thoughts and emotions, especially during a conflict. Instead of keeping your emotions inside, learn to talk about what is bothering or upsetting you. If you don't, your feelings will get bottled up, and you will explode with anger at the slightest inconvenience.

There are many feelings that people experience every day. Are you aware of all of them? There is joy, anger, sadness, confusion, gratitude (feeling thankful), and nervousness. You'll experience other emotions, and you might not know what they are or what they are called. Come up with your own names so you can easily express yourself.

In other words, you should always speak up about your thoughts and emotions. Even if you can't find the right words, invent your own. Speaking up is a great way to control and regulate your anger.

For example, your little brother breaks one of your toys. Instead of yelling at him, calmly say, "I am upset with you because you broke my toy. Please be careful with my things next time." This will make you feel better and prevent unnecessary fighting.

Now, check these interesting techniques that will teach you to speak up and express yourself.

61. The Gestalt Empty Chair Technique

The Gestalt Empty Chair technique is very effective and has taught many people how to express their thoughts and emotions. It is a very simple technique where you sit in front of an empty chair and imagine the person you want to talk to sitting on it and having a conversation, once as yourself and once as the other person.

Instructions:

1. Spend a few minutes thinking about who you want to talk to and what you want to say to them.
2. Take a few deep breaths to relax and focus.
3. Imagine the person you want to talk to sitting on the chair and start talking to them and using their name. Have a real conversation, like you are actually sitting with them.
4. Say everything on your mind, and switch chairs after you finish.
5. Take a few deep breaths again and imagine becoming the other person. Try to sit and talk like them.

6. Respond to the things you said earlier.

7. After you finish, return to the first chair and think about everything that was said.

8. If you have more to say, speak up and don't hold anything back.

9. Keep the conversation going until you feel better.

62. Talk to Your Angry Monster

Instructions:

1. Whenever you feel angry, draw how you think your angry monster looks at this moment.

2. Take a good look at the angry expressions on its face.

3. Ask it, "Why are you so angry?"

4. Pause for a couple of seconds, then answer the question as if you are it.

5. After the angry monster (you) tells you what is bothering it, take a couple of minutes and think about everything it told you.

6. Smile, look at your angry monster, and promise that things will get better.

7. Draw how you think your angry monster looks after the conversation. If it still looks angry, something is still bothering you. Keep talking about it until you can draw it looking happier and closer.

63. Express Yourself in Single Words

Instructions:

Agitated, Aggressive, Angry, Annoyed, Anxious, Bitter, Blue, Bored, Brave, Calm, Cheerful, Confused, Content, Cranky, Cross, Delighted,

Depressed, Determined, Disappointed, Distressed, Disturbed, Down, Ecstatic, Elated, Excited, Exhausted, Exhilarated, Fine, Friendly, Frightened, Frustrated, Funny, Furious, Gloomy,

Grumpy, Happy, Hurt, Intrigued, Irritated, Joyful, Merry, Miserable, Sad, Sorrowful, Tearful, Unhappy, Upbeat, Upset, Weak, and Weary.

1. Circle all the ones that apply to you, and ask your parents for their meanings if there are words you don't understand.
2. After you finish, write them down on a piece of paper and read them out loud.
3. Whenever you feel upset or angry, do this exercise to put your feelings into words. You will have the right vocabulary to communicate how you feel to other people.

64. Express Yourself in Pictures or Scribbles

Instructions:

1. Think of what you are feeling at this moment, whether anger, sadness, or fear.
2. Draw a picture that reflects your feelings. Either draw yourself or something associated with this feeling. For instance, if you are angry, you can draw an angry face or something that makes you angry.

3. Take a few minutes to look and think about your drawing. Then, ask yourself how you are feeling now.

65. Use Toys and Puppets

You can struggle with speaking up and expressing your emotions to your parents, siblings, or friends. Using a toy or a puppet will make the process easier since it will act as a shield you can hide behind while expressing yourself. In other words, it is the puppet doing the talking, not you.

Instructions:

1. Take a puppet or any toy of your choice.
2. Go to your parents, siblings, or whoever you are upset with, and hold the puppet to your face.
3. Express all your feelings to them and make it seem as if the puppet is speaking on your behalf.
4. Try this technique wherever you want to speak up but are afraid.

66. Read and Learn

Instructions:

1. Pick a book that talks about feelings or where the main character experiences various emotions (your parents can help you with the book choice).
2. Read the book and pay attention to how the main character behaves and feels in different situations.
3. Answer these questions:
   - What was the main feeling the character experiences?
   - Do you think this feeling is good or bad?
   - How did the character act when they were feeling that way?
   - Did the character express their feelings in a good or bad way?
   - When was the last time you felt like this character?
   - Draw something that reflects this feeling.

67. Feelings Collage (a bunch of pictures all together)

Tools:

- Glue sticks
- Scissors
- Poster boards
- Old magazines
- Markers

Instructions:

1. Build a feelings collage by cutting out pictures that express a variety of emotions.
2. Using a marker, write down each feeling reflected in the pictures.
3. Explain your collage and the different emotions in the pictures to your parents.
4. Observe the facial expressions and body language in the photos and discuss them with your parents.

68. How Would You Feel If?

Instructions:

Look at these different scenarios and answer how you would feel in each one of them.

How would you feel if:

1. Your mom yells at you.
2. Your sibling plays with your toys without your permission.
3. Your classmate laughs at you.
4. Your parents pick you up from school and take you for ice cream.
5. Your grandmother makes your favorite dessert.

6. Your best friend gets you a nice gift for no reason.
7. Your teacher criticizes your schoolwork.
8. Your parents punish you.
9. You lose your favorite toy.
10. Your friends and family throw you a surprise birthday party.

69. Map of Your Heart

Tools:

- Coloring crayons
- Piece of paper

Instructions:

1. Assign colors to different emotions.
2. Color the heart depending on each emotion you are feeling. Maybe you might assign blue to sadness and purple to confusion. If you feel mainly sad, color a big part of the heart with blue. If you are a little confused, color a small part with purple, and so on.

70. Journaling

Every night before you go to bed, write down all the different feelings you experienced throughout the day.

Don't only rely on chairs and toys when learning to express yourself. These techniques are only meant to get you started and relieve some of those nasty, heavy emotions that get stuck inside your body if you don't express them. However, if you are facing a serious issue like bullying or abuse, speak to your parents, teacher, or any adult immediately.

Angry Monster Checker

HOW ANGRY IS YOUR MONSTER RIGHT NOW?

☐ ☐ ☐ ☐ ☐

| Extremely angry | Fairly angry | Not sure | A little angry | Not angry |

Section 8: Changing My Story

Do you love stories? You aren't alone. Everyone loves a good story. In fact, many people have inner stories going on inside of them. They are usually based on your past experiences or how you understand certain events. However, sometimes, they can be negative thoughts that turn into *personal beliefs*. A personal belief is an idea you have about yourself or the world around you that you believe to be true.

For instance, if you believe no one likes you, you will misunderstand other people's behavior. Say you go to your best friend's birthday party, and she introduces you to her big sister. The sister says "hi" and walks away. You convince yourself that she doesn't like you and will tell your best friend not to talk to you again. You allowed your negative thoughts to create a false story – and you believed it. However, you find out later that the sister was having a bad day . . . that's the only reason she wasn't friendly to you.

Your brain can control and change the negative stories and beliefs through something called *reframing*. Thought reframing is replacing negative thoughts with positive ones. When you change the way you think, you change how your brain works. In time, positive thoughts will replace negative ones, and you will start thinking positively.

In this section, you'll find fun and easy activities to learn to reframe your thoughts and change your story.

71. Negative Belief

Write a negative belief, then rewrite the sentence in a positive way.

72. Draw Fear

Draw a fear, then make it funny.

73. Limiting Belief

Create a cardboard or Lego fence with your limiting beliefs on it, then knock it down.

74. Story

Write a story where you are the main character and have a magic wand that can change your life. Describe the three things you would change.

---

75. Name Three

Name three things and three people you are thankful for.

People

Things

---

76. Positivity Collage

Make a collage, fill it with happy and positive quotes, and hang it in your room.

77. Let It Go

Write down something negative or upsetting that has recently happened to you. Express all your feelings and write how sad or angry you were at this moment. After you finish, tear up the paper and throw it away.

78. What Do You Like About Yourself?

Write down three things you like about yourself.

----

79. Things You Are Good At

Write down three things you are good at.

----

80. What Do You Like About Your Life?

Write down three things you like about your life.

Angry Monster Checker

HOW ANGRY IS YOUR MONSTER RIGHT NOW?

☐ ☐ ☐ ☐ ☐

| Extremely angry | Fairly angry | Not sure | A little angry | Not angry |

Section 9: Creative Habits for a Calm Mind

Creativity is one of the most fun ways to express your feelings and thoughts. You don't think about other people's opinions; you are just enjoying the freedom of creating something you love. Creative exercises will make it easier for you to deal with your anger and negative thoughts and emotions. Instead of feeling sad or mad, you will calm yourself down by drawing, meditating, or repeating *affirmations* (saying words out loud that are good and positive).

You should practice these activities every day and make them a part of your daily routine. The word "routine" can sound boring, but do you know that having a routine can make you more independent? You will have your own habits that you practice every day by yourself without the help of a grown-up. You will also learn new activities and try new things that you may really enjoy!

This chapter will include fun and creative activities that you can practice daily to keep you calm and in control of your anger.

81. Daily Meditation

Instructions:

1. Sit in a comfortable position or lie down on a pillow or a blanket.
2. Close your eyes.
3. Breathe in and out deeply and feel how your body relaxes with every breath you take.
4. Focus on your right foot and notice how it feels at this moment.
5. Squeeze your right foot tightly to make a fist with your toes. Your foot should feel tense.
6. Hold this position while taking two deep breaths.
7. Next, release the tension from your foot all at once, not gradually.
8. Relax your feet and feel the tension that leaves your foot. Expect to feel a tingling; it is normal.
9. Take another long and deep breath.
10. Focus on your left foot and repeat the previous steps.
11. Move up to every part of your body and squeeze it until it feels tense/tight, then release while following the same breathing pattern in the previous steps.

The body parts you should focus on:

- Feet
- Ankles and calves.
- Knees
- Thighs
- Hips
- Butt
- Belly
- Chest
- Arms
- Hands
- Shoulder
- Neck
- Face
- Do your whole body at once

82. Daily Affirmations

Affirmations are positive phrases you repeat to yourself that can transform your negative thoughts into positive ones. Write them on sticky notes and place them in different parts around the house, like in your bedroom, bathroom mirror, and fridge. You can also put them in your lunch box to read at school and in your diary to read before bed.

- I am safe.
- My parents or teachers are here with me, keeping me safe.
- I am amazing.
- I am an important person/I matter.
- I can think positive thoughts.
- I can get through anything.
- I choose love over anger.
- I deserve love.
- I am grateful for everything I have.
- I am enough.
- I am capable of anything.
- I am a good friend.
- Today will be wonderful.
- I am a superhero who can do (conquer) anything.

- It's okay to make mistakes.
- I transform my anger into peace.
- I choose to be calm.
- I am a peaceful person.
- I release my anger.
- I am letting tranquility fill my heart.
- I control my emotions.
- I can tell my anger to leave.
- I can handle anything.
- I can solve my problems.
- Everything is great.
- I love myself for who I am.
- I think positively.
- I am in control of my own happiness.
- I will start my day with positive thoughts.
- A great thing will happen today.
- I feel calmer with every breath I take.
- I believe in myself.
- I am proud of myself.
- I forgive myself for all the mistakes I have made.
- I learn and grow from my mistakes.
- I am a kind person who helps other people.
- I can't control other people's actions, but I can control my reactions.
- I am excited about the future.
- I can find humor in everything in life.

83. Daily Visualization

Instructions:
1. Sit or lie down in a comfortable position in a quiet room with no distractions.
2. Pay attention to how you are feeling right now.
3. Breathe in through your nose and release the air through your mouth.
4. Repeat the previous step and feel your body relax.
5. Keep breathing deeply and slowly.
6. You are breathing in calmness and breathing out anger.
7. Visualize a place that makes you happy, calm, and comfortable. It can be a place you have been

before, like your grandmother's house, or a place you want to visit one day, like Disneyland.

8. Imagine every detail of the place as if it's real, like the smell, noise, and people around you.

9. Feel your body getting comfortable. You are enjoying the weather and your surroundings.

10. Stay in this place and imagine yourself either playing around or sitting still.

11. You feel safe and relaxed.

12. Suddenly, you see a large, strange-looking ball.

13. You slowly approach it to find that it is your negative thoughts.

14. So you unbutton your shirt, revealing your superhero suit.

15. You fly over the ball to the other side of your imaginary place.

16. You have managed to escape your negative thoughts.

17. Take a moment to enjoy and celebrate your victory.

18. Stay in this feeling for a while, and when you are ready, take a deep breath, count to three, and open your eyes.

84. 3-Step "Positivity Routine"

Instructions:

You can practice these three easy and fun steps every morning after you wake up.

1. Stretch.
2. Affirmations.
3. Jump three times while smiling.

85. Positivity Challenge

Instructions:

- Replace every negative thing you say about yourself with a positive statement.

- Do one thing that makes you happy every day, like eating your favorite food.

- Play with your siblings or friends in your garden or backyard every day.

- Dance to your favorite song.

- Make someone happy.

- Do something that makes you proud of yourself.

- Watch your favorite cartoon or a TV show that makes you laugh.

- Spend time with your pet.

Simply make it a habit to do something positive that makes you happy every day.

86. Give Compliments

Making other people happy can make you a calm and balanced person. Every day, put a smile on someone's face by giving them a compliment like,

- You look pretty today.
- Nice outfit!
- You have a nice smile!
- You played well today!
- Thank you for being there for me.

87. Received Compliments

Instructions:

1. Write down all the compliments people give you in your diary.
2. Read them every night before bed. This will improve your mood and boost your self-esteem.

88. Read a Story Before Bed

Read an inspiring story every night before bed. Reading is a great activity that will keep you focused and relaxed.

89. Practice Yoga

Instructions:

1. Stand on one leg while extending the other one backward.
2. Bend the upper part of your body forwards.
3. Extend your arms in front of you.

90. Play Music/Sport

Doing an activity you enjoy every day can make you happy and calm. Learn a sport or a musical instrument and make it a habit to practice either of them each day. Playing a sport will also boost your energy, which will, in turn, put you in a better mood.

Angry Monster Checker

HOW ANGRY IS YOUR MONSTER RIGHT NOW?

☐ Extremely angry   ☐ Fairly angry   ☐ Not sure   ☐ A little angry   ☐ Not angry

Section 10: Letting Go of Anger for Good

Do you remember the name of the song Elsa sang in the movie "Frozen"? You are probably singing it right now, "*Let it go,*" since you sang it in a previous exercise. Have you ever wondered what the title of this awesome song means?

Letting go is putting all your bad memories, negative thoughts, and everything that bothers you behind you. You aren't constantly thinking about the past or worrying about the future. You are letting go of everything that makes you unhappy or angry. You understand that some things are out of your control, and there is no need to worry about them.

Letting go is choosing to forgive yourself and the people who hurt you. Even if they don't apologize, you forgive them for the sake of your well-being. You release yourself from the anger and the pain they caused you.

These people will always control you and live in your head until you let them go. Forgiveness sets you free since you won't waste your time and energy thinking of what the other person said or did.

Forgiving yourself is equally necessary. You are young and still learning. Naturally, you will make mistakes. Learn from them, then let them go. Treat yourself with kindness and understanding.

Happy people are the ones who don't hold grudges and can forgive and forget. When you forgive yourself and others, you release negative emotions and anger and become a calmer person.

Use the fun activities below to learn how to let it go!

91. Ho'oponopono Prayer

Ho'oponopono means to make things right or to bring balance, and it is an ancient Hawaiian prayer that encourages forgiveness. It consists of a few words you can repeat to yourself daily.

I am sorry.

Please forgive me.

Thank you.

I love you.

92. The Printable Balloon Activity

Instructions:

1. Bring a few balloons and write on them the things you want to let go of, like negative thoughts or the names of the people you want to forgive.
2. Go outside and release these balloons.

93. Letting-Go Meditation

Instructions:

1. Sit in a comfortable position and close your eyes.
2. Breathe in deeply and feel your body relax as you breathe out.
3. Think of the thing or person you want to let go of.
4. Clear your mind. Only focus on what you are letting go of and notice how you feel.
5. Name the emotion this thought stirred up, like anger, frustration, sadness, or resistance.
6. Notice which part of your body is stressed by this thought, like your legs, arms, neck, or head.
7. Be fully aware and present with this sensation and sit with it.
8. Sit with this feeling for as long as you need, whether it's one minute, ten, or more, until it goes away.
9. Once you feel at peace, slowly open your eyes.

94. Flushing Negative Thoughts

Instructions:

1. Write down a negative thought or emotion on a piece of toilet paper or draw something that expresses how you are feeling now.
2. Throw the tissue in the toilet and flush it!

95. The Worry or Negative Thought Eater

Instructions:

1. Create a worry eater using a tissue box, crayons, and other supplies.
2. Write down or draw your negative thoughts or the people who upset you on a piece of paper and feed it to the eater.

96. Basketball

Instructions:

1. Write down all the things that upset you on a basketball.
2. Each time you throw the ball, you are letting go of your anger and negative emotions.

97. Negativity Jar

Instructions:

1. Write down the things you want to let go of on small pieces of paper.

2. Visualize releasing all the negativity in the jar; they will be trapped once you cover it with a lid.

98. Talk to Your Toys

Instructions:
1. Tell your toys about all the things that annoy or upset you.
2. Believe that the toys will take away these feelings and set you free.

99. Candle Exercise

Instructions:
1. Close your eyes and imagine yourself blowing candles.
2. With every breath you let out, you release negative emotions.

100. Send a Letter to Your Anger Monster

Instructions:

Write a letter to your anger monster, telling it why you don't need it anymore without closing the door, as anger may be needed when you have to defend/protect yourself and others.

Angry Monster Checker

HOW ANGRY IS YOUR MONSTER RIGHT NOW?

☐   ☐   ☐   ☐   ☐

| Extremely angry | Fairly angry | Not sure | A little angry | Not angry |

Bonus Activity: Check Your Emotions! (Checklist)

Now that you have learned everything about anger and the best exercises to keep you calm and in control of your emotions, this last activity will provide you with a list of questions you can print out and use whenever you feel angry, stuck, frustrated, or irritated. After you finish answering the questions, you can learn how strongly you feel from one to ten, identify the emotion/thought, and confront/overcome it with one or more of the exercises from the book.

Activity #101

1. I understand what anger is and what triggers this emotion.

   • Yes

   • No

2. I know why I get angry.

   • Yes

   • No

3. I am familiar with my anger monster.

   • Yes

   • No

4. I now know how anger expresses itself.

   • Yes

   • No

5. I can befriend my anger.

   • Yes

   • No

6. I know where my anger comes from.
    - Yes
    - No

7. I understand the role my emotions have in impacting my anger.
    - Yes
    - No

8. I understand how my thoughts affect my emotions.
    - Yes
    - No

9. I know the different types of thoughts.
    - Yes
    - No

10. I understand the power of negative thoughts and how they can make me angry.
    - Yes
    - No

11. I acknowledge my negative thoughts and understand why I have them.
    - Yes
    - No

12. I know what fear is and how it affects my thoughts and emotions.
    - Yes
    - No

13. I know the difference between healthy fear and unhealthy fear.
    - Yes
    - No

14. I believe I can control my anger.
    - Yes
    - No

15. My anger has no control over me; I control my anger, monster.
    - Yes
    - No

16. My thoughts have no control over me; I am the one in control.
    - Yes
    - No

17. I feel that I can speak up and express myself.

- Yes
- No

18. I am aware of my inner story.

- Yes
- No

19. I know how to reframe my thoughts to change my personal beliefs and story.

- Yes
- No

20. I have the tools to lead a calm life and control my anger.

- Yes
- No

21. I can let go and forgive myself and others.

- Yes
- No

22. I am aware of all the blessings I have in my life and am grateful for them.

- Yes
- No

23. I can identify negative thoughts and emotions and am fully equipped to overcome them.

- Yes
- No

24. I understand how my anger can affect the people in my life, and I am willing to change.

- Yes
- No

25. I understand now there are better ways to handle my anger that won't cost me my relationships.

- Yes
- No

Assess your answers. Repeat the exercises in section ten if you are still struggling with letting go. If you don't like your inner story, refer to section eight. If speaking up is still an issue, go back to section seven.

Angry Monster Checker

HOW ANGRY IS YOUR MONSTER RIGHT NOW?

☐ ☐ ☐ ☐ ☐

| Extremely angry | Fairly angry | Not sure | A little angry | Not angry |

Conclusion

You did it! You finished this book and are on your way to changing your life and being a calmer and happier person. This book provides all the information you need to understand your anger and the reasons behind it. You met your anger monster and learned that the only way to regulate this emotion is by befriending it.

Now you understand that your anger comes from negative emotions and thoughts. If you are aware of your thoughts and emotions, you can control your angry responses. You also learned that fear greatly impacts how you feel and think.

The activities in this book were fun, easy, and beneficial. In time, you will notice how your life is changing and that you have become a calmer and happier person. You will be the one in control of your thoughts, emotions, and anger. You will grow, change, and be the best version of yourself.

Thank you for finishing this book! Hopefully, you found the exercises and information helpful and felt their impact on your life. Buying and reading this book shows you are serious and committed to changing yourself. You are on your way to awesomeness, so keep going!

References

(n.d.-a). org.uk. https://www.mind.org.uk/information-support/types-of-mental-health-problems/anger/causes-of-anger/

(n.d.-b). choosingtherapy.com. http://choosingtherapy.com/types-of-anger/

10 activities for teaching young children about emotions. (2021, january 26). brookes blog. https://blog.brookespublishing.com/10-activities-for-teaching-young-children-about-emotions/

10 types of anger: what's your anger style? (2019, february 17). com.au. https://lifesupportscounselling.com.au/resources/blogs/10-types-of-anger-what-s-your-anger-style/

5 reasons why it's important to forgive. (nd). psychology today. https://www.psychologytoday.com/us/blog/in-flux/202009/5-reasons-why-its-important-forgive

5 visual ways to help children to let go of nagging thoughts. (2018, april 3). mind-and-seek. https://www.mindandseek.com.au/post/5-ways-to-help-children-to-let-go-of-nagging-thoughts

anger monsters. (nd). therapist aid. https://www.therapistaid.com/interactive-therapy-tool/anger-monsters

binns, d. (2023, march 13). challenging negative thoughts: 20 top activities for learners of all ages. teaching expertise; dontan. https://www.teachingexpertise.com/classroom-ideas/challenging-negative-thoughts-activity/

cherry, k. (2013, august 2). emotions and types of emotional responses. verywell mind. https://www.verywellmind.com/what-are-emotions-2795178

cirino, e. (2018, december 3). anger management exercises: 9 exercises to help curb your anger. healthline. https://www.healthline.com/health/anger-management-exercises

coach, c. l.-g. e. (1585300190000). rewiring your brain to think differently – yes you can change your thoughts and way of being. updated technique. linkedin.com. https://www.linkedin.com/pulse/rewiring-your-brain-think-differently-yes-you-can-change-langston/

cook, a. (2019, may 1). 4 steps to befriending your anger. dr. alison cook. https://www.dralisoncook.com/befriending-your-anger/

crossland-otter, a. (n.d.). fighting fear and negative thoughts. mht. https://www.mentalhealthtoday.co.uk/blog/therapy/anxiety-fighting-fear-and-negative-thoughts

cunningham, c. (2023, february 7). 25 activities to boost positive attitudes in elementary school. teaching expertise; dontan. https://www.teachingexpertise.com/classroom-ideas/positive-attitude-activity/

deciphering anger: what it's trying to tell you. (2017, january 25). pine rest. https://www.pinerest.org/newsroom/articles/deciphering-anger-blog/

do, e. m. (2019, december 2). what exactly does letting go mean? – the startup – medium. the startup. https://medium.com/swlh/what-exactly-does-letting-go-mean-195ee294a4e0

domb, a. (2020, february 26). the stories we tell ourselves –.the beautiful truth. https://thebeautifultruth.org/life/identity/stories-ourselves/

dormoy, m. (2019, august 29). kids' guided relaxation: pausing to understand anger. green child magazine. https://www.greenchildmagazine.com/guided-relaxation-pausing-to-understand-anger/

dulin, d. (2021, march 31). 144 proven affirmations for anger to calm you down. unfinished success. https://unfinishedsuccess.com/affirmations-for-anger/

elveru, e. (2020, september 11). 3 meditations to help little kids handle big emotions. parents. https://www.parents.com/health/mental/meditations-to-help-little-kids-handle-big-emotions/

enger, b. (2021, january 31). 30 day positivity challenge – change your life and your mindset! positivity pledge. https://www.positivitypledge.com/30-day-positivity-challenge-master-healthier-habits-in-30-days/

expressing emotions through drawing. (2015, september 25). k-12 thoughtful learning. https://k12.thoughtfullearning.com/minilesson/expressing-emotions-through-drawing

forgiveness: letting go of grudges and bitterness. (2022, november 22). mayo clinic. https://www.mayoclinic.org/healthy-lifestyle/adult-health/in-depth/forgiveness/art-20047692

fritscher, l. (2008, march 15). the psychology of fear. verywell mind. https://www.verywellmind.com/the-psychology-of-fear-2671696

gillette, h. (2022, october 7). why am i always angry? causes, signs, and more i. psych central. https://psychcentral.com/blog/angry-all-the-time-for-no-reason-this-might-be-why

goldman, r., & young, a. (nd). affirmations: what they are and how to use them. everydayhealth.com. https://www.everydayhealth.com/emotional-health/what-are-affirmations/

guided imagery and meditation for kids. (2012, august 15). health powered kids. https://healthpoweredkids.org/lessons/guided-imagery-for-younger-children/

healing our hearts and the world through ho'oponopono. (2020, october 31). xmonks; team xmonks. https://xmonks.com/healing-our-hearts-and-the-world-through-hooponopono/

how to use meditation for anger control. (2022, september 15). bettersleep.com. https://www.bettersleep.com/blog/how-to-use-meditation-for-anger-control/

keri, c. (2019, july 9). affirmations for kids who worry. counselor keri. https://www.counselorkeri.com/2019/07/09/affirmations-for-kids-who-worry/

kids, p. (2018, february 27). how to raise kids who can speak up. pbs kids for parents. https://www.pbs.org/parents/thrive/how-to-raise-kids-who-can-speak-up

ls pearce – making friends with anger: how anger serves us. (2021, february 4). ls pearce. http://pearcetherapy.com/how-anger-helps-us/

lacroix, m. (2021, march 19). how to make friends with your anger. molly lacroix – author | author of restoring relationship; molly lacroix. https://mollylacroix.com/how-to-make-friends-with-your-anger/

learning about thought reframing. (nd). alberta.ca. https://myhealth.alberta.ca/health/aftercareinformation/pages/conditions.aspx?hwid=abk7438

lodge, g. w. (2020, march 27). 22 best yoga poses for kids in 2023. great wolf lodge family fun. https://www.greatwolf.com/blog/yoga-poses-for-kids/

lonczak, h. s. (2020, december 24). how to express your feelings: 30+ emotional expression tips. positivepsychology.com. https://positivepsychology.com/express-emotions/

lorelle. (2018, august 31). how to let go- the only technique you will ever need. lorelle dehnhard; lorelle. https://lorelledehnhard.com/how-to-let-go-the-only-technique-you-will-ever-need/

lorina. (2023, april 17). using temper monsters to help children take control of their temper. com.au. https://aussiechildcarenetwork.com.au/articles/child-behaviour/using-temper-monsters-to-help-children-take-control-of-their-temper